SEAN BELL
JUST 23

Thoughts from a Mother in Spoken Word by Kisha Walker

Valerie M. Bell

FOREWORD BY REVEREND AL SHARPTON

authorHOUSE®

AuthorHouse™
1663 Liberty Drive
Bloomington, IN 47403
www.authorhouse.com
Phone: 1 (800) 839-8640

Published by AuthorHouse 08/19/2016

ISBN: 978-1-5246-2158-2 (sc)
ISBN: 978-1-5246-2156-8 (hc)
ISBN: 978-1-5246-2157-5 (e)

Library of Congress Control Number: 2016912274

Print information available on the last page.

Library of Congress Cataloging-in-Publication Data
Bell, Valerie M.
Sean Bell: Just 23: Thoughts from a Mother in Spoken Word by Kisha Walker
Valerie M. Bell, co-author Kisha Walker, Foreword by Rev. Al Sharpton.

p.cm
Summary: "Sean Bell: Just 23: Thoughts from a Mother in Spoken Word by Kisha Walker, co-
author Kisha Walker, Foreword by Reverend Al Sharpton, is a reflective account of the final days
of Sean Bell, and the subsequent agony of a mother's grieving heart." —Provided by co-author

The following is a true story; however, some details have been omitted and some names have been substituted to protect privacy.

This book is dedicated to
William G. Bell Sr., William G. Bell Jr., Delores Bell,
Nicole Paultre-Bell, Jada Bell, and Jordyn Bell,
who have endured in this most intimate tragedy.
May this book be a comfort to your mind, heart, and soul.

Table of Contents

Never say goodbye; always say "See you later."

—Sean Bell

Foreword

One of the greatest challenges in life is dealing with death. The unanswered questions, the pain, the immense sense of loss never truly go away; rather, you learn to carry on through that grief. In March of 2012, I buried my mother after she lost her long battle against Alzheimer's disease. As difficult as that experience was, it was natural; a child is supposed to say goodbye to a mother or father when that time arrives. What is unnatural is for a parent to bury their own flesh and blood. That is a unique anguish that no one but that mother or father will ever comprehend. Valerie M. Bell carried that burden when the son she brought into this world was viciously killed in an act of senseless gun violence. And to add agony to her heartache, those responsible for Sean Bell's death were the ones who were sworn to protect and serve.

I had the opportunity to know Valerie through the worst of circumstances. As we marched and rallied for justice for Sean, her dignity never wavered. Even when many tried to demonize her son after death, she held her head high and pushed forward. Valerie serves as an example to mothers all over this country and around the world. And Valerie is an example to all those who have faced injustice of the highest degree but found inner peace and strength to humbly carry on even when others attempted to stop them. But she would not stop, could not stop, and did not stop because Valerie's spirit only knows truth and justice.

Throughout my life, I have interfaced with people from virtually every aspect of society. But I can tell you that nothing amazes me more than the sheer will and power I have discovered in folks like Valerie. Even in the midst of unimaginable cruelty, she found the ability to forgive—but never forget. Her fight for righteousness and fairness continues daily so that others will not have to endure the pain and suffering that she and her family went through.

The following pages are a window into Valerie's heart, mind, and soul. We can all learn a thing or two from this remarkable mother. I for one am honored to have walked alongside her on the long journey towards justice.

Reverend Al Sharpton
Founder and President
National Action Network (NAN)

Author's Note

Our son will never be forgotten. Your sympathetic hearts and selfless efforts of support have confirmed this to our hearts. Thank you for suffering with us, crying with us, fighting for change with us, and keeping vigil with us in hope that this will never happen again. Always remember this:

God will always get the glory while Sean Elijah Bell gets his rightful story.

—Valerie M. Bell

But let justice run down like waters and righteousness
as a mighty and ever-flowing stream.

—Amos 5:24 (AMP)

Introduction

Just 23 will take you on a journey of the days that followed the fifty shots that were blasted by New York City police officers, resulting in the murder of Sean Bell. Valerie Bell finds herself having to regroup and reconnect with her emotions. Her poignant recollection, as revealed to her goddaughter Kisha, gives an account of a mother's heart that is ripped opened and filled with distress over the loss of her child.

Through her deep, spiritual conviction, Valerie weaves a story filled with scriptures about the day that the world remembers: November 25, 2006, the day her son Sean, at the young age of twenty-three, a young man celebrating at his bachelor party in the early morning hours on his wedding day, was murdered.

The shock rang through the community. The screams, the crying, the anger, and disbelief shook the community of Southeast Queens, communities throughout the boroughs of New York City, and, in fact, the world. Through the snow, the rain, and the hot sun, the people marched, sat in vigils, appeared at the courthouses, and supported countless TV and radio appearances. To continue his legacy of giving, the Sean Elijah Bell Community Center opened its doors in Jamaica Queens, New York, on May 18, 2011.

Valerie Bell's faith is her legacy to us. We celebrate this woman, who is more than a conqueror through Jesus Christ. We celebrate her strength, her wisdom, and her transformation into the woman God intended her to be.

Patricia Hogan-Currie
The Sean Elijah Bell Community Center

Co-Author's Note
Black Rose

The New York City Police Department handed Valerie Bell a black rose. This rose was unique. It had fifty petals. As this rose blossomed, each petal became darker than it previously appeared. This rose had four jagged-edged thorns, and its stem was a blade. Years later, Valerie Bell is still holding this rose. You see, the black rose is the death of her son Sean Bell.

The fifty petals are the fifty shots surrounding his death. The darkness of each petal represents the insensitive lies and defamation of character created to justify the undignified actions of the New York City Police Department. The four jagged-edged thorns are the three New York City police officers who fired the fatal shots and the judge who turned a blind eye to *justice*. The stem is the verdict of acquittal.

The pages that follow offer a glimpse into the intimate process of healing. The journey into the darkest parts of each petal will bring Mrs. Bell to a place where she will no longer suffer under the piercing sting of the stem.

Kisha Walker
Co-Author

Chapter One

My Story

Wedding Bells

I will never forget October 30, 2006.

It was a Monday and Sean called me to say, "Ma, I'm ready to get married."

I remember this day like it was yesterday. I *knew* this had to be God. Prior to his epiphany, Sean had attended his sister's choir concert at the church that Sunday. I asked Sean when the wedding was, and he gloated, "November twenty-third."

Intrigued, I whispered, "Why that date?"

He replied, "It will be our six-year anniversary."

I didn't want to ruin his fantasy, but I had to tell him that Thanksgiving Day fell on the twenty-third that year. That might make it difficult to schedule a wedding. Holding on to hope, I told him that I would call Bishop Lester Williams in the morning. I hung up the phone and thought to myself, *I know he didn't mean this November!*

I had to be sure, so I called Sean back. "What year are you planning to marry her?"

He said, "Ma, this year!"

All I could say was "Wow!"

True to character, Sean never saw obstacles as defeat. If he wanted it, he was going to make it happen. It was as if he didn't even see the challenge in planning a wedding in only three and a half weeks.

Then he said to me, "Ma, I want *her* mother and sister to pick out the dress."

I felt the burn of tears welling up in my eyes. *My son is getting married,* I gently thought in my heart.

After a minute of silence, I finally asked, "Do you know that there isn't enough time to get a place for a reception?"

Sean persisted, "Ma, I got this. All I want is the family to be there—my father as the best man, my brother, William, and a few friends."

I called the bishop the next day to find out if he would be available to perform the wedding ceremony on Thanksgiving Day. The bishop agreed, but it would have to be scheduled for 9:00 a.m. in his office. I relayed the news to Sean. After I explained the conditions that Bishop Williams gave, Sean's response was simple. "Ma, you *know* she won't be ready at that time!"

We brainstormed for a moment, and then Sean decided and said, "Let's make it for that Saturday, November twenty-fifth."

At this point, Sean and I alone knew of his wedding plans. I remember thinking how different it was for a groom and the mother of the groom to plan the wedding.

"When are you going to let *her* know about your wedding plans?" I asked.

He enthusiastically blurted out, "I want to surprise her!" His answer surprised me!

I couldn't help myself, and I bellowed, "Now, how are you going to surprise *her*?"

He responded, "All I want is for *her* to go down to the courthouse in enough time to get the marriage license; then *she* would go to the place where the reception will be."

'*Young love*', I thought to myself. I sympathetically encouraged him, "Sean, that is so romantic, but we need to find a place—and *she* needs to find her own dress. Honey, every bride wants to pick out her own dress; and don't forget, we are only working with three-and-a–half-weeks' time."

Sean agreed, "Okay, Ma, I will propose to *her* and tell *her* the plans I have for our wedding day."

Here is the hand of God in the midst of it all, I thought. At work the next day, I told a co-worker that Sean was ready to get married and that I was trying to find a place for his reception. My co-worker mentioned La Bella Vita on Rockaway Boulevard in Ozone Park. I immediately called the establishment, and lo and behold, they had the date! They confirmed a room that would hold one hundred people was available from 7:00 p.m. until midnight on November 25, 2006.

All I was able to say was, "Thank you, Jesus!"

Just as Sean had confidently insisted, "Ma, I got this," I knew in my heart that God would be in the midst of it all.

The wedding plans moved forward, until …

The Day Before His Last

As time was winding down from weeks into hours, the challenges of planning a wedding in such a short time began to arise. It was now the day before the wedding, and I was settling down for the night. I had just told Delores to wrap her hair tight and to go to bed when I received a call from Sean around 10:00 p.m. He was a little upset after receiving phone calls from his aunts in the South who were disappointed about not receiving invitations to the wedding. I listened intently as he spoke. I could hear the hurt in his heart and my heart was opened to him. When he finished speaking, I explained why I didn't send the invitations. I told Sean that I had spoken to his aunts concerning the wedding invitations. I figured with the short timeline, the trip to New York would have been expensive for them.

After hearing my explanation, Sean said, "Ma, you're right."

I knew Sean had plans to go out with his father and brother that night. I asked him if he was going to pick up his brother, and Sean replied, "Ma, I will call you back."

I would never receive that phone call.

I called my husband to see if he was going to pick up William, our eldest son. He explained that he was waiting to hear from Sean. After speaking to my husband, I drifted off to sleep. About an hour later, William called me. He asked me if I'd heard from Sean.

I said, "Yes, he hasn't called you yet?"

"No" he replied.

I told William to come home and rest for the wedding tomorrow; he agreed. I remember saying to William, "Maybe it wasn't meant for you to go." I drifted off to sleep again. Hours later, I awoke to see my husband coming into the bedroom. I asked him if he had been out with Sean.

He said, "Yes, I just left him not too long ago."

These words were spoken to me between 4:00 a.m. and 4:20 a.m. I drifted to sleep again.

The Phone Rang

My cell phone rang between 4:30 a.m. and 5:00 a.m. The frantic voice said, "Mrs. Bell, you have to come to the hospital! Sean is in the hospital!"

My very first thoughts were, *Oh God, he was in a car accident!* I began to pray. When we arrived at the hospital, we saw a crowd of people standing outside the emergency room. My husband and I were escorted to a waiting room by hospital security. As I followed the officer down the corridor, I struggled to keep hold of my faith. My heart had fallen into my stomach, and my knees buckled underneath me. Since I worked for the hospital, I knew that when security escorts a family to a private room, the news wouldn't be good. Inside the room was Sean's fiancée, her sister, her mother, and a host of other people.

Sean's fiancée was crying uncontrollably. "Sean has been shot by cops fifty times!" she said in a panic. Her words shattered me like glass, and I fell to my knees crying and screaming.

"No, God, no!" I can't remember feeling such agony; I was lost in an abyss of despair. It was a feeling too great for my body to harness. I continued to scream. I remember wailing, "Mommy, Mommy, please take care of him!" My mother went home to glory on August 13, 1988. I *knew* she would watch over him. At that moment, my mother was my only tangible connection in which I could see a small relief of solace. Believing that Sean was with her helped me to balance the *new* reality of separation;I remained in this life, and Sean, now, resided in death. *This is how his life ends?* I thought, *No good-bye? No forewarning of this closing door? Just an untimely grave?*

I wanted to see him. No, I *needed* to see him, but I wasn't allowed to because of the police investigation. Still down on my knees, all I could do was hold myself as I cried. *This can't be happening*, I thought. *He is getting married today at 7:00 p.m.*

I was in disbelief. All I could do was to keep going; I had to keep moving. I kept the hair appointment I had made for the wedding. As I sat in the salon, I was filled with numbness, lingering agony, disbelief, and a deep pain I wouldn't allow to surface. I asked God, "What went wrong? Why my son? He was just about to turn his life around."

Chapter Two

Thoughts from a Mother in Spoken Word by Kisha Walker

Fifty Shots

*I will go before you and level the mountains
(to make the crooked places straight).*

—Isaiah 45:2 (AMP)

*I will not in any way fail you nor give you up nor leave
you without support.*

—Hebrews 13:5(AMP)

"I love you" were the last familiar words I spoke before crossing the threshold of chaos that would lead me to a dimension where a new life awaited—a life I did not choose. It was four o'clock in the early morning hours of November 25, 2006. The voice on the other end of the phone was disturbingly frantic as the words "Sean is in the hospital!" were uttered through the phone line. As my husband and I shuffled out of bed, grasping for clothes, my mind quickly conceived a safe-haven thought for me to hide in.

Car accident, I thought. It was in that very thought I remained—until I reached the hospital and heard the words *fifty shots.*

Cock and reload ...

Those fools were on a mission, that alcohol had their souls, had their minds spinning, filling their thoughts with illusions, drawing conclusions of situations which were mistaken, and they end up taking the innocent life of Sean Elijah Bell. And to hell with their reasons for seizing and ceasing his life, standing as the judge, deciding that day he would never take a wife. And his daughters' lives, they changed forever, to be filled with suffering the pangs of a father slain. Slain with no wrong on his hands the night his life was claimed, marked for death, fifty shots at best. As that moment unfolded, all five lost their souls, adding insult to injury, the cock and reload ...

Now a community joins together for a family torn apart by five souls passing judgment to stop an innocent man's beating heart.

Sean

For I know the thoughts and plans that I have for you, says
the Lord, thoughts and plans for welfare and peace and
not for evil, to give you hope in your final outcome
—Jeremiah 29:11

I let out a long, deep sigh.

W. H. Y.

These three letters have paraded through my mind for seemingly endless years. Like an inconsolable child screeching at the very peak of her voice, I too screech, *"Why, Why, Why? Why, Sean?"*

In the form of a man, with the spirit of a dove. Having the heart of a lion, being blessed with eyes of an eagle and favored with the covering of love. This picture of unspoken contentment was my son Sean. Beautiful in features, he was very kind to the eye. With morals deeply seated from the proper teachers, he was a gentleman, not just some guy. Life's experiences bore him stripes upon his back, though being born a black male in America guaranteed him that. Soft-spoken, soft-hearted, like a lamb he'd come to me. Resting his head upon my breast, he would speak to me about dreams and simple things: baseball, his family, the new things his eyes would see. But the day would come when his simple dreams would cease to be. My child upon my breast, in his love, our love rests untouched, permanently etched into the creases of life past. As I try to silence thoughts, my mind will struggle no more to hold what is not lost because it lives perpetually in eternal lore.

Unusual Rain

Who gives rain upon the earth and sends waters upon the fields, so that He
sets on high those who are lowly, and those who mourn He lifts to safety
—Job 5:10–11 (AMP)

I will never forget December 1, 2006. The benediction had ended. Sean's funeral was over. I can distinctively remember that as I prepared to leave the church, I experienced this most unusual feeling. It was sublime. This feeling took over my emotions; it focused and stabilized them. The doors of the church opened, and there it was: rain. Rain literally poured out of the sky, as if a thousand angels were crying. It was the most *unusual rain* …

The silent darkened sky displayed overwhelming storm clouds hovering in an atmosphere of saturated sorrow. The moment I feared the most was prepared. The time had come. The earthen bed prepared for the grave is lifted by men with heavy hearts. I, suspended between two dimensions, reality and dream, followed the procession to the open door of the hearse. Light out of darkness emerged, as your Beautiful was placed into the moment. The windows of heaven were opened. The fallen rain was filled with the melodies of new life and blessings that would lessen the sting of death, sorrow, and angered fear. The summation of Sean's death was transformed into hope, not yet seen, in this most unusual rain.

Fallen Ash

He has covered me with ashes

—Lamentations 3:16

December 2, 2006, was the day Sean's body was lowered into the ground. My mind whispered to me, *He will be just a box full of ashes.* As if the moment were created to shatter what was left of me, the only words I was able to form into sound were "Oh God, why me?" I thought I would succumb under the weight of the pain that filled my mind, body, and soul. The epiphany hovering before me forced me to accept the reality that I would never hug, see, or hold my baby son again. My days were reduced to *fallen ash …*

A plethora of dried, gray ash suffocates the continuum that stretches between brokenness and healing. Ash has fallen on the untouched path I have yet to tread. It is thick, like a tear, saturated with the heaviness of emotion. Thick, like the inhuman stench of the irrevocable injustice of the cock and reload. Thick, like the thickness of the breaths I held each time I had to digest the reality being thrown before me. Your beauty is the light that leads me through the darkness that placed itself within me in the place where you used to be. I fight hard, Sean, to trust the Lord in spite of what I feel. I fight hard to love in spite of it. I fight hard not to collapse into the bitterness that stalks my every thought. I fight hard not to succumb to myself. Ash, light like wind yet heavy as three thousand fallen angels before God. Gray ash, the present hindrance before my eyes that already has me defeated. It is only the Lord's love that enables me to endure.

In My Thoughts

My Son, keep my words; lay up within you my commandments
(for use when needed) and treasure them.

—Proverbs 7:1 (AMP)

After leaving the cemetery, all I could do was think about you, wondering what I could have done to save you. The words *Don't go—come home* cascade through my mind. What could I have told you that night that would have altered your ultimate fate? My thoughts remain unanswered. I knew you wanted to savor the last moments of your bachelor life. Every unspoken word from that night resides silently within *my thoughts …*

I wrap you in purple, surround you in a bed of lilies, and water you with my love. I call you Beautiful. You are a bright light, the twinkle in my eye, the dream come true in my heart. Sean, you are all these things to me and more. I adore your memory. I await my complete strength to look back on the days when I held you in my arms, spoke to you in your teenage years, encouraged you in your adult life, and blessed you with wisdom for your wedding day. Though tears may drop—I miss you so much—and sorrow weighs thin, Beautiful, I know I will see you again.

The Strength of Love

I have strength for all things in Christ Who empowers me
(I am ready for anything and equal to anything through Him Who infuses
inner strength into me; I am self-sufficient in Christ's sufficiency).
—Philippians 4:13

The above scripture has helped strengthen my children throughout the years, even to the present day. I can remember a time when Sean was having challenges finding a job. Although he faced opposition, my faith in his eventual success was unshakable in his situation. He knew I wouldn't let him give up. Just as God had given me unconditional love, Sean knew I had the same love for him and his siblings. He was a witness to the many days I labored, putting my children before myself. Sean knew it was this very scripture that strengthened me. I thank God for the enduring strength given to me to love my family. I thank the Lord for *the strength of love.*

The strength of love will crush the walls of hell within you, shatter the shackles you've placed upon your own hands, and bind you to the very people you claim to hate. The strength of love has kept me from falling into diverse levels of uncommon hypocrisy, known to destroy from the inside of the soul and to manifests as the death of the spirit. Compassion is the unquenchable desire of man. It ultimately allows mercy to cover the weakness of flesh. Weakness can overtake a man in his ignorance and cause him to perform unspeakable things, leading to unspeakable pain in others even indirectly involved. Thus it was with the officers who took the life of my son Sean Bell—a life they didn't create and had no reason to hate yet destroyed all the same. Faced with a two-edged sword enlarged in the center of my chest, I search for the compassion that manifests as mercy—mercy that, at times of reminiscing about Sean, seems to have run empty. When justice and revenge hold the same weight, when hope and trust battle like the forces of good and evil, I remember His word: "I was shown mercy so that in me the worst of sinners, Christ Jesus might display his unlimited patience as an example for those who would believe on Him and receive eternal life." 1 Timothy 1:16 (NIV)
And in that I rest.

Déjà vu

David said, While the child was still alive, I fasted and wept; for I said,
Who knows whether the Lord will be gracious to me and let the child live?
—2 Samuel 12:22 (AMP)

I had a forewarning in my spirit. I had this feeling something bad was going to happen. I made sure to pray for traveling mercies for my son every time he left the house. I would worry, I would call, and I would reach out to everybody who knew him, just to make sure he was all right.

He would say to me, "Ma, I got this. Do what you do best."

He knew I was always praying for his well-being. It was as if the energy of my worrying could be felt. Family and friends would report to me every time they saw Sean in passing. It was an additional reassurance to me that my prayers were being heard. Then one day, it all came back to this feeling. On November 25, 2006, at 4:56 a.m., the forewarning instantaneously morphed into my worst fear. And without further warning, *déjà vu …*

One time was incomprehensibly mind-numbing.

In truth, I haven't even tried to accept this with human understanding. The separation that formed between my mind and body I call a miracle blessing. Slowly, gently, and ever so carefully this event is opened before me. Silently struggling for soul peace from the tormenting revelation of an unbearable truth, I find myself stuck in déjà vu. My every thought is reminiscent of you, Sean. My child, your smile, your death, it's true! They killed my son! The men in blue! I can't do this! The anger in me rises up so strong! This feeling of hate tries to overtake the soundness of my mind, and this is wrong! Then all at once, my emotion is gone—until the next thought begins, and there I'll be, helplessly stuck in déjà vu again.

A Mother's Womb

Behold, children are a heritage from the Lord, the fruit of womb a reward.
—Psalms 127:3 (AMP)

You were born of me on May 18, 1983, and my womb held no sorrow. Twenty-three years later, my womb cries out from the snatching away of your life. I clutch my belly and cry out for the comfort of my own mother. I cry out from the agony of my empty womb ...

Brought forth of my womb, your presence still abides. It internally fills me with the multiplication of who I am. Blessed and favored, I bore from within me a man. I nurtured you, raised you, prayed for you, and let you go to live in this world. The word of God that was sown in you continued to govern you. Time passed, your life progressed, and you held the balance of life like a battle wound upon your chest. Then from deep within me, so silently, my womb began to groan. The agony of the empty. Your presence no longer roams. My womb, it bleeds. I can taste it with the beating of my heart. Each heartbeat pronounced my mourning and my yearning for the presence of my son. The bleeding continues; my mourning has progressed. In time, my son, I'll grow to endure the deepness of this emptiness.

In My Mind's Eye

... hold tightly to what you have until I come.

—Revelation 2:25 (AMP)

As I lay at night with my eyes closed, my thoughts are still of you. With my eyes tightly shut, I can see a clear picture of your bright smile and your glowing eyes. Sean, I never want your image to end, though I know that once I open my eyes, you will disappear from reality again and back into my mind's eye until we meet again …

I surround you within me, and every facet within you I can see. Although memories of you are all that I have, I embrace each of them with the strength of my mourning, and I feed them with the weight of my love. In my memories you are vibrantly beautiful and funny. You are as real as the breath that I breathe and as tender as your memory. Sean, the tears that flow from me bear your name. This life that I now live has changed its form. It will never be the same. I continue on, for my time here is not yet complete. With my heavy heart, I am constantly at the Lord's feet, weeping, resting, searching for understanding, and pondering what will be. So, I will continue to surround you within me. I will embrace you with my mind's eye. I'll etch your face into the life that's perceived only by my eyes, a life that is complete and sublime. If only for a moment, we can be in the same space and time, even if it's only in my mind's eye.

Silver and Gold

I have a private treasure of gold and silver which
I give for the house of my God:
—1 Chronicles 29:3

To think of silver and gold is to think of something that holds great value. Sean left behind an abundance of memories that my family treasures. I graciously thank the Lord for my granddaughters Jada and Jordyn. In my life, they are as valuable as *silver and gold.*

One child was too young to remember; the other child will never forget. Emptied of her life's joy, she searched for answers to the questions of a grieving child. Jada, in her young maturity and with deep confusion and sorrow, questioned her father's absence. Jordyn's father-daughter relationship with Sean exists through pictures and stories alone. How do you explain to a mourning child that the negligent responsibility of the city holds the accountability for her father's death? Silver and gold deposits of a father's love are buried deeply within their souls. Silver: Jada bears her father's face, his teachings, and his mind. Gold: Jordyn, to whom belongs her father's legacy, each story he has left behind.

Beneath

Listen to my words, O Lord, give heed to my sighing and groaning.
—Psalms 5:1 (AMP)

Sean was the one who could see beneath it all, the one who was strong, with an old mind and soul. He was able to discern when something was bothering me. He could even see beneath my smiles. He would encourage me by saying, *"Ma, do what you do best."*

"What would that be, Sean?" I would ask.

He'd reply, *"Just keep praying."*

Deep, unidentifiable groans rise within me as I ride past the landmark that holds the story of my son's death. Someone told me that time heals all wounds. Instead, though it has been years, it seems as if this wound I was chosen to receive has deepened. It transcends past my three-dimensional being. I cry without sound. My tears are of one meaning. I suffer under the thoughts of "What if." These are the things you don't see. They are hidden within me.

· *A Mother's Love*

Let everything you do be done in love
(True love to God and man as inspired by God's love for us).
—1 Corinthians 16:14 (AMP)

A mother's love is unconditional, as God's love is for us. I can remember staying by your side when you were sick in the hospital. I remember calling all over town for you when you didn't come straight home from school. I can recall trudging through a snowstorm, in the early morning hours before church, to reach your job to inform your supervisor that you had the flu. These are the things *a mother's love* will do.

As pure as new life budding upon a tree in the crisp early months of spring, so are the earnest pleas of a mother's love. She prays for the protection of her son's soul. Constant, countless prayers she has offered up to God as the world begins to unfold. The world's desire was to separate his spirit from the seed of life the Lord had rooted within him. Conscious decisions and consequences shared the same timeline and had their place. The mother's fear was subdued. In the midst of her torment, she was comforted. Her son's soul returned to the Father; his body returned to the ground. Though her world was shattered, her trust in the Almighty was sound. Time passed, and her pain became profound. Her tears revealed the secret weeping of her womb, the relentless ache in her heart, the empty echo of absence, and the unwavering endurance of a mother's love.

I Miss You

and you will be missed, for your seat will be empty.
—1 Samuel 20:18

Love is an energy that fills the existence of life.
Your life was strong. It remains the same.

I feel you all around me, watching me. Your presence is so strong my eyes see you, yet they don't. My mind embraces you, and my heart still beats for you. Your daughter bears your face and your beauty. The baby has your energy; it's amazing! Sean, you left me too soon. I miss you. As I continue to walk through life, I know you walk with me. My heartbeat echoes your footsteps; my love still calls your name. Your absence has profoundly changed me. I will never be the same.

Platinum

*"The reward of humility and the reverent and worshipful
fear of the Lord is riches and honor and life"*
— Proverbs 22:4

When I think back to the relationship you and your
father shared, it reminds me of the platinum effect.
The chemistry and connection were indescribable.
Whatever choices you made in your life, your father was proud.
From baseball to fatherhood, and one day becoming an electrician,
you worked hard in all you put your hands to do.
Since you have passed on, your father now works for you,
letting your platinum effect shine through.

*In silence I crown you with platinum. I respect the man you had become.
I admire you for the unselfish choices you made. At the age of twenty-three you
walked responsibly in the morals our family upholds. I watched you fulfill all
the expectations I had dreamed of for you. You are to me a classic, an entity
filled with humble confidence and authentic generosity. You were my friend.
Life has become a challenge in ways that are unfamiliar to me. Time has
intensified the pain; you occupy my every thought. Your death brings forth an
unnatural agony no amount of time can erase. I may never accept the fact that
your life is done, yet it has been an honor to call you my son.*

Field of Gold

*Be still and rest in the Lord; wait for Him and
patiently lean yourself upon Him …*

—Psalms 37:7

In the memory of our fallen son, we held a fifty-day vigil. The purpose of the vigil was to show America that neither our family nor our community would forget what happened to our son. Each morning for fifty days, arriving at 4:56 a.m., I sat in front of a banner that displayed Sean's face surrounded by fifty bullet holes. Each bullet hole was individually numbered.

It was a disturbingly vivid reminder to see day in and day out. My mind would wander into a serene escape. I would think of Sean in a field of gold enjoying life. I imagined how life would be if things had not changed. After moments that seemed like eternities, a compassionate voice saying "Good morning" would jolt me back to reality.

Sitting in the silence of the fields of gold, I gaze down at the copper-colored wheat and inhale the absence of sorrow. The fragrance of answered prayer lifts me into a cloud of worship. I surrender to the sovereign peace of acceptance. I have chosen to embrace you in the evolution of our relationship. I have chosen to suppress the thought of not embracing you at all. I sit here, Sean, in the beauty of your memory …

I Love You

We love Him, because He first loved us.
—1 John 4:19(AMP)

"*I love you,*" was a sentiment we often shared. It was alive, and it was true. In the midst of all that has happened, I still love you. I'm grateful for the time I had with you, even though it was only twenty-three years.

Early morning dewdrops moisten the endurance of my faith. Golden rays of hope cultivate the mineral-rich soil where green pastures of healing grow. The fragrance of reciprocated love filling the atmosphere in the midst of paradise, at the East Gate of Beautiful is where I find you. I love you.

Sequential Love

Your faithfulness continues from generation to generation ...
—Psalms 119:90(AMP)

When I am sitting at my desk or walking to a destination, I will suddenly get what I call a "Sean break." A flash of Sean comes to mind, and tears begin to well up in my eyes. I'll have an emotional moment, but with a smile I begin to think of the *sequential love* he left behind, a sweet memory of unselfish love.

Perfection, evenly blended with affection, is the core nucleus of our family's longevity. Never minus one, yet there has been a sudden multiplication of the spirit of our son, which has become the substance known to us as sequential love. He has become a powerful crescendo that's heard in our family's presence. It is a crescendo that is as sweet as musical notes melodically orchestrated and composed by the strength of his core. Musical inspirations from the loveliness of her who endured the mourning of a child. The mixture of keys and chords, accumulating into a fierce impact of explosive emotions, mirrors the ruggedness of life. Suddenly it tapers off into a serene melody known to us as sequential love. It has become the legacy of our family.

Bearing

Take (with me) your share of the hardships and suffering
(which you are called to endure) as a good first-class) soldier of Christ Jesus.
—2 Timothy 2:3(AMP)

Bearing this existence without you has been hard. I have sustained the memory of you to pull me through. I see you in Jada and Jordyn. I see you in their smiles. I see you in their faces and in their personalities. Sean, I still suffer a void, but love *bears* up under all …

Bearing the beauty of suffering and reaping, time serves no purpose in being, yet it is vital just the same. Salted and deeply rooted are the wounds of my sorrow. Time has not pardoned my pain. It merely surrounds me with flames of compassion, which has sustained the current pressure of healing while I bear existence without you.

Presence

Do not cast me away from your presence, and do
not take Your Holy Spirit from me

—Psalms 51:11(AMP)

The *presence* of your life made someone smile; from the homeless man on the street you stopped simply to say hello, to your family, your friends, and the community that has embraced you. Sean, your absence is felt.

The emerging of a new leaf from the womb within itself brings to mind the beauty of the circle of life. Life is perpetual, and death is but a necessary phase. A doorway leading into elevated dimensions of life forms not easily recognized. Death is, however, life nonetheless. It confirms the truth of your existence inside of me. Your memories are the footsteps left behind as you travel into new life and abide in new forms; yet, somehow your presence remains the same.

Effect Change

the Lord will come (as unexpectedly and suddenly) as a thief in the night.
                                        —1 Thessalonians 5:2 (AMP)

My life has changed since the death of my son. My husband regards me as the "Ambassador of Justice and Peace." I have always walked with a silent demeanor, until "they" stole my son's life like thieves in the thick of darkness and *effected change.*

Effect Change has become my branded name, effective as a fire ignited by a single flame. The spark was created by my burning rage brought on by the death of my son, who died at the hand of ignorance holding a gun, ignorance dressed in blue, ignorance who took a pledge to protect me and you. Betrayed while in a haze that alcohol creates, facing a state of hate, on his wedding day my son was slain. Injustice was elevated to heights that equaled the seats of magistrates, with lawyers trying to portray the humbleness of those dressed in blue. Pleading nonsense, they tried to make it make sense to you and I—as if we were blind and void of the ability to comprehend murder and cruel intent. As their delusion was projected as protection, the truth was severed in two, yet we continue to stand until justice reigns through. The mistaken judgment of men changed the life we know, changed it with the cock and reload. They will reap what they have sown. The silent war between the unprotected and the law will only surrender to peace and unity when we effect change.

Let Your Light Shine

Make Your face shine on Your servant;
Save me in Your lovingkindness

—Psalms 31:16(AMP)

The doors of the Sean Elijah Bell Community Center were opened May 21, 2011. Our vision for the center is to be a safe haven for the neighborhood children and a helping hand to the community. You were a beacon of light, and we continue to let your light shine.

Authoritative beauty beholding the very essence of who you are, colorless yet colorful, your image remains tucked away in my heart. It remains in a place not far from the hope that emanates from the evolving blessing that you are and have always been to me. A glimpse of true light catches my eye, and in the simplest things I can see you. As the spirit transcends barriers that the flesh cannot, your death has the ability to infiltrate minds of darkness. Your life changed its form, and the greatest love came forth. Sean Elijah Bell, let your light shine.

Sean Bell Way

In the *fields of gold* there was an *unusual rain* bringing your *presence* in *the strength of love. It* was displayed to me in *platinum, silver and gold,* letting *your light shine in my thoughts. In my mind's eye, beneath fallen ash,* are *fifty shots* that *effect change* in *a mother's womb. A mother's love* in *faith and thanksgiving* says *thank you. I love you, Sean.*

Chapter Three

The Family's Love

Thoughts from Sean's Mother

Hurt, pain, tears, fear, sacrifice, sorrow, numbness, emptiness, the void of Sean. As these emotions rapidly overwhelmed my mind, I asked Kisha, my goddaughter, co-worker, and friend, to write a book of Sean Elijah Bell. I wanted it to be my thoughts in spoken word. If it were not for his birth, life, and death, this would not have been possible. I thank God for Jesus, who gives me strength to keep standing as a humble, steadfast, unchanging woman of God. I'm believing:

**God will get the glory
while Sean Elijah Bell gets his rightful story.**

Thoughts from Sean's Father

"My son is great. My son lived honestly. He will change the world. God chose him. I'm going to miss him. Everyone is going to miss him. I will be my son from now on, I am working for him!"

—*William G. Bell Sr.*

Thoughts from Sean's Daughters, Jada and Jordyn

Daddy, I will always know there is no one like you.

No one compares to or can do what you do. I will always know how special you are; you light up my world and shine like a star. I will always know that you are still here with me standing by my side. So you can see I will always know how much you love me. I'll always remember to be the best I can be.

—Jada

I love him so much I want to pray for him because he passed away. He said "You will always be my little girl." He flew up in the air and said "I love you." I love him so much.

—Jordyn

Thoughts from Sean's Brother

Sean was my best friend. I can still remember Sean following me around, wanting to do everything I did. Even though we were five years apart, we did almost everything together. We shared toys, played with the same friends—we would even play baseball in the house. I'm proud to say that I taught Sean how to play baseball. He found an incredible love for the sport that took him to many huge platforms. My parents always had us in organized sports, in church, or on vacations. My brother will always be in my heart. Gone too soon, but I thank God he was in my life.

—William G. Bell Jr.

Thoughts from Sean's Sister

At the time you left me, I thought it was a dream. I didn't believe it. All I could think was, *This is just make believe.* All I heard was crying, yelling, and the words "Why me, why me?" Why did I have to be the person that lost someone like you? Why did I have to be the one to lose a person that had dreams just like me? Why did I have to hear on television that it was fifty shots that killed you? Why me? Why can't I *still* believe this is true? Why do I have to live each day thinking *Why you?* Only God knows the truth. It's been many years since you've been gone, gone forever in reality but never in my heart. You will never be forgotten, Sean Elijah Bell. I love and miss you!

—Delores Bell

Chapter Four

Love from the Sisterhood

You Are Me, and I Am You

This is dedicated to the mothers who have endured the loss of a child by the hands of those who were sworn to serve and protect.

In a blink of an eye, an ordinary moment in time, our paths became intertwined, woven, stitched together by sudden loss in our lives. You are me, and I am you, perhaps with different measures of burdens and pain, yet it's pain all the same.

I suffered with you, and you suffered with me.

Now time has gathered us together to draw strength in our unity.

Mrs. Diallo

When a mother loses her child, half of her becomes void; she will never be whole again. Valerie Bell and I share this sentiment, the loss of our sons at the hands of those who were suppose to protect them. As parents, if we could chose, we would choose to pass on before our children. If they were suffering from an illness, we would find the best cure to heal our children. A mother who dreams that she can undo any harm that comes to her child dreams fruitlessly. The one last thing she can do is to try to give her child back his story. The greatest and least obligation she can fulfill.

In a poetic tone, Valerie Bell has given her son Sean Bell back his beauty and dignity. Reading this book will make you feel the power of true love from a mother to her child and the need to change the senseless brutality towards innocent young black men in America.

Kadiatou Diallo
Mother of Amadou Diallo
Author of *My Heart Will Cross This Ocean*

Constance Malcolm

Dear Mrs. Bell,

I would first like to thank you for giving me the opportunity to read your excerpts. I would also like to express that the author did an excellent job in conveying your experience in such a wonderful way, where I felt as if I was reliving his moments with you. To that I say, "Thank you to the author."

I would like to share my personal thoughts on your book. I believe you expressed your passion about your son and the wonderful times you and the family were looking forward to before his horrible death. I also believe that you were able to send us back to the night the crime occurred and what he was doing up until that moment. I would have loved to know how his new life would've been. You did such a wonderful job explaining the major change in his life and how he was looking forward to raising his family.

It is sad to know that our worlds were joined by the actions of NYPD officers, and not in a good way. It is sad to know that we were forced to become victims of society, with the horrible nightmares that we constantly suppress. I believe that your love and trust in God is stronger than anything, hence the downpour of rain on the day that God called your son home. The acceptance of no longer having your son will be the cross to bear. The realization of the fact that he was taken by the ones we told our children to trust will never be accepted.

Through the expression of your feelings and telling the story of your son and his death, I can only hope that you will inspire myself and other mothers who have fallen victim to the hands of NYPD to do the same.

Thank you,
Constance Malcolm
Mother of Ramarley Linden Graham
Born April 12, 1993
Died February 2, 2012

Wanda Johnson

Just 23

The author, Valerie Bell, writes a gut-wrenching true story about her son who was killed by NY police officers. This true story takes you step by step through what happened to her son. Filled with emotion and pain, the author recalls all that happened up to the time of her son's death. How the groom prepares for the bachelor party that evening, a night of rejoicing and joy. Then, suddenly, everything changes. What was an evening of laughter turned into tears; the preparation for a wedding turned out to be the preparation for a funeral of the author's very own son. A day of celebration turns tragic. You will feel what the author feels after reading her vivid accounts. Your emotions will be on high, you will find yourself happy at first, ready for the celebration, and then you will find yourself full of hurt, sadness, and tears. Crying and feeling the pain the author feels as if it was your very own child. Finally, you will begin to ask, why did this happen?

The author understands and is a God-fearing woman who believes that there is a season for everything. So this season in Valerie's life she knew she would have to share with the world what happened at "Just 23." Valerie has been thrown out to the forefront to send a message of hope to others who have lost their relatives to gun violence. After reading this book your life will never be the same again. You will be prompted to take action and want to work to change laws regarding racial profiling.

From one mother to another mother, I can sympathize with Valerie. I understand the pain that the author endured. When she cries, I cry with her, knowing the unfathomable pain that the author feels.

Wanda Johnson
Mother of Oscar Grant III
killed at age twenty-two January 1, 2009
by a BART police officer in Oakland, California

(The award-winning movie *Fruitvale Station*, winner of the Grand Jury prize at Sundance Film Festival in 2013, shows what happened to Oscar Grant and other young men who have been targeted.)

Chapter Five

Sean's Final Farewell

Sean Bell's Obituary

Sean Elijah Bell
1983–2006

On Wednesday, May 18, 1983, Sean Elijah Bell was born to William Gabriel Bell and Valerie Shepherd Bell at LaGuardia Hospital in Queens, NY. From an early age he was very special and destined for greatness. He accepted Jesus Christ at twelve years old and was baptized by his great-uncle Rev. Charles Walker at St. John's Baptist Church, Jamaica, NY. When he was seven his parents recognized Sean's love for baseball. He started playing with the Wakefield Ozone Park Little League. He had an outstanding gift for the game. At eighteen, his high school baseball team won the championship at Yankee Stadium. Sean was a dominant pitcher in the Public School's Athletic League. As a result of his efforts, after graduation, he went on to pitch for Nassau Community College. Although people had doubts about Sean's potential of becoming a professional player, his father never gave up on his dreams. Until this day, Sean and his father had a special bond that no one quite understood.

Sean fell in love with the mother of his children. He had chosen her to be his wife, and his plan was to surprise her with a wedding. Unfortunately for him, they couldn't get married without her knowing about it in advance. On Tuesday, November 14, the couple met with Bishop Lester Williams to discuss their wedding plans. They were scheduled to do a public wedding ceremony on Saturday, November 25, 2006, at 7 p.m.

Unfortunately, the earthly ceremony never took place. Sean was killed early that morning in a senseless hail of gunfire by the hands of New York City police officers. He is sorely missed by all who loved him.

The Eulogy by Bishop Lester L. Williams

Photo Credit: Michael Nagle

Eulogy for the Late Sean Elijah Bell

Grace, mercy, and peace be unto you from God our Father and our Lord and Savior, Jesus Christ. I greet you in the joy of Jesus, who even in this climate of adversity and extreme emotional duress, that His joy still gives us strength. I honor my distinguished spiritual comrades who share my work on the gospel battlefield, the elected officials and community leaders who represent the various offices and levels of our local, state, and federal government, the official staff and constituency of the Community Church of Christ International, to my son and daughter in the ministry, William and Valerie Bell, to one of our newest members, Nicole Paultre-Bell, the entire Bell family, my brothers and sisters in and out of Christ, and to the aggrieved local, national, and international communities. My condolences to the Dorismond and Diallo families as their pain is rekindled. They thought it not robbery to come today to support you and share in your pain and grief because they have been through this before. My task, which is very difficult, is to bring words of comfort in a time of a grave injustice. You cannot fathom the events of this week and the toll that it has taken on all of us. But it's because of His joy that gives me strength to say to this family, and to this congregation, that God is still a good God. That will not mean anything to those who do not share our faith, because you don't understand that goodness is a quality of God, which is not changed because of adverse situations. Ask not for whom the bell tolls. The bells are tolling for Sean. The bells are ringing outrage and will not stop ringing until justice prevails. In the words of Dr. Martin Luther King: *"Injustice anywhere is a threat to justice everywhere."*

A few days ago, Thanksgiving bells pealed the air as joyful hearts gave thanks to God for all things. In a few weeks to come, Christmas bells would celebrate another season of thanks for the birth of the baby Jesus. On Saturday, November 25, weddings bells were to pierce the silence of a subdued relationship and give way to laughter and great joy. But instead, in the middle of these celebrations, fifty shots were heard around the world that disrupted and shattered our field of dreams. In lieu of joy and laughter, there are tears of sorrow and heavy hearts. We are the faithful, and the spirit of God in us will not let us mourn as one without hope, for our hope is in Christ Jesus. What do you say that can make any sense out of this horrific tragedy? A tragedy is where there is an awful twist of fate and what is supposed to be happy turns out to be sad all because of a tragic flaw. The tragic flaw is fear, fear from the police for us, and fear of the police toward us. This tense climate makes for a very volatile state of affairs. All week long, reporters have asked how does one cope with this, and what do you say to the family? I say to them what I have said to hundreds before, that Jesus will sustain us in this hour. He will keep you if you want to be kept. Scripture is clear. "Blessed are they that mourn for they shall be comforted." Simply put, if you mourn, you will be comforted, kept by God. He is not in the business of explaining why things happen. That's His permissive will. But He is in the business of sustaining us when things do happen. That's His divine will. There are witnesses in this very room who will concur with me that God will keep you in perfect peace in the midst of this terrible storm. That will not mean anything to those who do not share our faith, because you don't understand that goodness is a quality of God which is not changed because of adverse situations.

As people of faith, we are mandated by the very principles of God's word to forgive others of their debts and their trespasses. When we forgive, there is a release, and it makes it easier to stop hurting. We must pray for the Guzman and Benefield families that have been touched by this tragedy. We must pray for the police officers, because they too are a part of this human fabric and network of change. May I caution you that because we forgive, that does not imply that we are passive and do not seek justice. I am angry as hell. But our anger must not cause us to sin. We seek justice on God's terms. This family and the entire constituency of this church, the people of this community and city collectively, concur that this is a heinous tragedy. But we are determined not to mar the memory of Sean and bring greater shame to our fair city with violence and dereliction in behavior. We must work on positive change. You must register to vote, because voting gives you a voice. We must be a part of the process in change. We do have an alternative to this dilemma. We are going to rise up and make this free nation and city respond to us with courtesy, professionalism, and respect. It is not just a slogan on the side of a car. But it must be a goal that we must equally work to achieve.

Romans 12:19: "Dearly beloved, avenge not yourselves, but rather give place unto wrath: for it is written, Vengeance is mine; I will repay, saith the Lord.

20 Therefore if thine enemy hunger, feed him; if he thirst, give him drink: for in so doing thou shalt heap coals of fire on his head.

21 Be not overcome of evil, but overcome evil with good."

We have been through this before, and we are overcomers. I know firsthand what oppression and injustice is. I was in the sixth grade at Caldwell Elementary School when an assassin's bullet took the life of then-President John Fitzgerald Kennedy on November 22, 1963. I was fifteen years old on April 4, 1968, when a bullet took the life of our drum major for justice, Dr. Martin Luther King Jr. in Memphis, Tennessee. Needless to say, I was devastated, crushed, and, moreover, afraid to grow up in a violent society and expect to be anything but another black boy from the projects of Mobile, Alabama. My mother instilled in me that I could be anything that I wanted to be and that I could do anything that I wanted to do. One day, to our surprise she bought a home, all by herself, and moved us to what was then an all-white neighborhood. I went off to college, returned home for school break, and I was arrested for trespassing. The officer explained to me that there were no niggers in that part of town. I told him that was true, and I agreed. But there is a black family that just moved in. Of course he did not believe me. I was incapacitated and terribly inconvenienced for a night in the Mobile County jail. That was almost thirty-five years ago. I have had encounters with the police since then and most recently this past August in upstate Schenectady; for driving a Mercedes after midnight, in what was termed as a "drug-infested neighborhood." Not all of us get our cars through the selling of drugs. We work to obtain the American dream, and there are some of us who are blessed of the Lord. The officer came to the conclusion that I was buying drugs when, in fact, I was having a diabetic episode. I was lost and made a wrong turn. The only drugs that I had in my possession were purchased over the counter at CVS or prescribed by my doctor. So you don't have to wonder why our blood boils and why we are angry. We are tired of the pattern and history of being profiled and being victims of mistaken identity. So here we are again knocking on the door of justice. This time, we win.

I was not a good student when it came to math, but one thing that I do know is that fifty is greater than twenty-three. While I was sharpening my mathematical skills, my mother was grooming my spiritual side. It's that side that reverses everything on the natural side. Over the years it seems like the natural side had dominated everything. It is true that in the natural, we are troubled on every side, yet not distressed; we are perplexed, but not in despair; persecuted, but not forsaken; cast down, but not destroyed; etc. You need to know that there is a bright side somewhere, a side greater is less, and less is greater. Fifty shots is greater than Sean's twenty-three years of life. Sean Bell died in a hail of bullets. He had a short name and a short life. But his death will forever be etched in the hearts and minds of every person in this room, and undeniably he will never be forgotten.

"Youth ages, immaturity is outgrown, ignorance can be educated, and drunkenness sobered. But stupid is forever." —Aristophanes

Every black male needs to capitalize on this death. It's time for you to be responsible for your future. The hip-hop community has not been vigorous enough in promoting your educational and social well-being. Instead it highlights drugs, sex, and the wild life because that's what sells. We advertise their culture and cause it to thrive. Since we like to advertise for the people who do the least for us, I want every man of color to get a T-shirt, a jacket, a baseball cap, whatever, and write the number twenty-three on it. I am not prejudiced against women. I am married to one. But without the man and his voice, there will be no future. Do what this young man was about to do. If you love her, marry her and take care of your children. He was twenty-three years old. Most men who are twenty-three do not want the responsibility of a wife and a family. At twenty-three most of us were just beginning to live. Spiritually, twenty-three is the number of death. It is the number of transition. The Bible teaches us that we all have a set time of departure. Wearing this number does not mean that you will die at twenty-three; however, it symbolizes that three is the number of resurrection. That's the first thing that will occur after death. We will be resurrected. Twenty is the number of redemption. After death, we will be redeemed. Redemption is God's saving activity toward mankind. In order for resurrection to be valid, one must have died. We have been born into a society where we are marked for death from our birth. Now it's time for you to live. I agree with Dr. King. "It does not matter how long you live, but how well you do it."

Verse 23 is the capstone of the text of Psalm 50. "Whoso offereth praise glorifieth me: and to him that ordereth his conversation aright will I shew my redemption, the salvation of God." The word *conversation* in this text is not your language or speech. Conversation means your way of life. Live your life in a way that is pleasing in the sight of God, and God's faithfulness to you is that I will not forget you in the end. Might I go a step further, since there are those who think that right living is all that you need? No, you need to accept Jesus as Lord of your life, and He will order your steps. My message for this younger generation and those that are under the sound of my voice is that you need to return to the basics. Live a life that glorifies God, a life that is meaningful. Although Sean lived a short life, it was a meaningful life, despite his record. Sean was not perfect, and neither are any of us. We have all sinned and come short of the glory of God. Therefore, when we repent of our sins, it does not matter if the newspaper publishes it, your friends tell it, or if the TV airs it; God will show us his salvation. He will rescue us from the perils of this world.

There is a situation that has occurred that is viewed as a grievous wrong, and the mayor, the police commissioner, the elected officials, and clergy alike cannot make it right with our policies and rhetoric. But as my grandmother said years ago, "There's someone that sits high and looks low and got all power in his hands." He sits high in the seat of justice and looks low in the path of unrighteousness and indignities, and He alone can and will make it right. All I have is my faith, and I will not allow this system to take it away. The blood of Jesus will prevail. We have every right to be angry. There is a qualifying condition. Be angry, but sin not. Jesus was angry enough to drive out the money-changers from the temple. What He did was overturn a system. Be angry enough to overturn a system through positive change. How long will that take? I don't know, because change is a process, and change will come. Each day we live, the seasons of life will come and go. But with each season there is change. I thank God for Sean, that his death will bring the change that we need to assure our future generation that they too can have life, liberty, and the pursuit of happiness in this free society. I am not talking about what the constitution says or the Magna Carta says. I am talking about what Jesus said in John 10:10: "I am come that they might have life, and that they might have it more abundantly."

I know that this appears to be another one of the darkest times in our lives. But I want you to be well assured that behind every dark cloud there is a silver lining. No matter how dark it gets, the sun will shine after while. Redemption is on the way. For everything that we have lost and every one that we have lost, justice may be slow, but I believe that she's on her way. I can see the light of her torch and the Bible in her hand while truth is marching on.

Luke 12:56: "Ye hypocrites, ye can discern the face of the sky and of the earth; but how is it that ye do not discern this time? 57 Yea, and why even of yourselves judge ye not what is right? 58 When thou goest with thine adversary to the magistrate, as thou art in the way, give diligence that thou mayest be delivered from him; lest he hale thee to the judge, and the judge deliver thee to the officer, and the officer cast thee into prison. 59 I tell thee, thou shalt not depart thence, till thou hast paid the very last mite."

The skies opened their eyes and cried today with this family and this nation. The weather is confused. It is December, and the temperature is rising. Tomorrow the winds will howl as the cold grave swallows the remains of this intended husband, father, son, and friend. As we leave the resting place, we leave knowing that this is not the end. Someone must answer for the heinous atrocities that have been leveled against the people of God. Saved or unsaved, we are the people of God. Jesus is clear in this parable that you are able to discern the weather, the temperature, the climate, things in the natural and in the physics of life. We are tempted to judge who is right and who is wrong. This is not about the judgment of man. This is about the judgment of God. He warns us not to become the judge, the jury, and the executioner. The adversary, the judge, and the officer in this passage of scripture are united in the person of God. The adversary charges us with our faults. The judge decides our guilt. The officer executes vengeance upon us for what we have done. So what makes us right? We are right only when we reconcile with God. This season in this city is designed to jump-start our monitor. There ought to be a monitor that appeals to our conscience that something is amiss. God assures us that He will deliver us from our doom. The debt of sin and injustice must be paid. Sean paid a debt. But his debt cannot cancel the debts of a sin-sick society. It is by divine executive order that we pay that debt here by throwing ourselves at the mercy seat of God. He is the only one that can change the leopard's spots, wash away our sins, equalize injustice.

I am saddened and disillusioned by what has taken place in the greatest city here on earth. I have not lost hope that redemption draweth nigh. I have hope in Christ eternal that these troubles will not last always. I have hope that there is a place besides this place where the righteous can call home. There is a place where the wicked shall cease from troubling. There is a place where the weary shall be at rest. There is another city where there's no night, no sickness, sadness, no sorrow. There is another great city where there's no more pain, suffering, crying, death. There is a place where there are those that have dipped their robes in the blood of the lamb and will come forth from the north, south, east, and west of Jamaica; Queens, Brooklyn, the Bronx, Staten Island, Manhattan; New York, the fifty states in the union; the world; etc. They will come crying redeemed, redeemed. I have been washed in the blood of the lamb, because my hope is built on nothing less than Jesus' blood and righteousness. I dare not trust the sweetest frame, but only lean on Jesus. It's on Christ, the solid rock, I stand. All other ground, foundations, and systems are sinking sand.

Fight the good fight of faith. Don't let your labor be in vain in the Lord. So tonight we die to the sins of this world and offer our praise unto God, because when we honor God, we glorify Him. Thank you, Valerie and William, for giving us Sean. We thank God for the life of Sean, and we thank God for his death; because it will bring change in the earth. I also thank God for His son, Jesus Christ, Who has brought change in our lives.

He changed us with His birth, and He changed us in His death. In the short thirty-three years He gave us on earth, He gave us access to everlasting life. He died a senseless death yet a necessary death to give us assurance of resurrection. It is a fact that they whipped Him, pierced Him in the side; blood came streaming down; He hung His head in the locks of His shoulder, and He died. It is a fact that the disciples wept for Him during His three-day stay in the grave. It is also a fact that weeping may endure for a night, but my Joy got up one morning with all power in His hands.

All week long reporters have been looking for a story.

(Isaiah 53:1) "Who hath believed our report? and to whom is the arm of the LORD revealed?

3 He is despised and rejected of men; a man of sorrows, and acquainted with grief: and we hid as it were our faces from Him; He was despised, and we esteemed Him not.

4 Surely He hath borne our griefs, and carried our sorrows: yet we did esteem Him stricken, smitten of God, and afflicted.

5 But He was wounded for our transgressions; He was bruised for our iniquities: the chastisement of our peace was upon Him; and with His stripes we are healed."

And because we are healed, I must report to you that I have a story, song, praising my savior, all the day long. This is my story! In the good time, bad, when I'm up, down, etc. Because of that assurance, he is absent from the body and present with the Lord. Therefore no runs, no hits, no errors. Just peace and joy. Peace and joy.

The funeral service of Sean Elijah Bell
Bishop Lester L. Williams, Senior Pastor
Community Church of Christ
December 1, 2006

Chapter Six

The Legacy of the Sean Bell Community Center

The Community Center—Olevia Campbell

To continue his legacy of giving, the Sean Elijah Bell Community Center was born on May 18, 2011. Out of this birth came new beginnings; a new legacy came forth. Solidified in her faith and vision, Valerie Bell knew she was not limited by resources, her family, or her background. God has equipped and empowered her. God has given her creativity, ideas, invention skills, and talent. Together with her husband, William Bell Sr., she will go forth with seeds of greatness.

—Olevia Campbell, cousin of Valerie Bell

The Closing of the Sean Elijah Bell Community Center

This year marks the seventh (7th) year of Sean's death. The number seven spiritually means "complete." As we enter into the eighth (8th) year of "New Beginnings," with God's mercy and grace, we seek God for new direction and guidance concerning the future of the Sean Bell Community Center. Our prayer is for God's presence to continue to abide in the midst of it all.

On November 22, 2013, the Sean Elijah Bell Community Center, after two years of serving the community, closed its doors. The overall objective for the center was to provide a safe haven for cultural and educational programs. We were privileged to be able to provide our Southeast Queens community with opportunity and hope through the programs we offered for adults as well as children six days a week.

We've had more than 150 children enrolled in various programs since our opening, with a majority attending our summer and after-school programs. The center also provided reading and math tutoring, GED preparation, social services, assorted recreational activities, arts and crafts, legal referrals, dance classes, exercise classes, and more. Our plan for the forthcoming year was to continue our present programs, introduce a new initiative where we will be offering Emergency Medical Training (EMT), and a Saturday itinerary, which was to include individualized tutoring, dance classes, and instructors to teach karate.

Above our hope is the Lord's will; where He leads we will continue to follow. Our hearts are steadfast towards the advancement and well-being of our community. We will be present and continue to help in any way we can.

In enduring love and respect,
Valerie M. Bell

A Word from Neville O. Mitchell

As one of the attorneys for the Bells, the father, William, and mother, Valerie, I have witnessed missteps, half steps, and steps fetched leaving no impressions. Death has revealed Sean's true potential—a larger-than-life figure. He is a public person.

His loved ones struggle with this development as people and causes foreign to them invoke his name. They are thankful for those who genuinely care and truly want to protect our youth. Though they ache for Sean— every mother's son—they know his light has revealed the injustices heaped upon our community. They soldier on in a life less normal in his absence with their faith as solace. The Bell peals for justice. Justice will be done.

—Neville O. Mitchell
Mitchell Law Office

Chapter Seven

Tributes in Pictures

Injustice

Photo Credit: Michael Nagle

Photo Credit: Bell Family

Photo Credit: Joan Williams
May 18, 2010: Sean Bell's street renaming at
Liverpool Street and Ninety-Fourth Avenue

Photo Credit: Kisha Walker
May 18, 2010, Sean Bell's street renaming at
Liverpool Street and Ninety-Fourth Avenue.

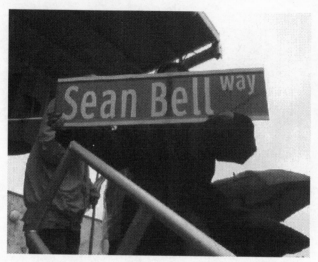

Photo Credit: Kisha Walker
May 18, 2010, Sean Bell's street renaming at
Liverpool street and Ninety-Fourth Avenue.

Photo Credit: Joan Williams
Photo Edit: Kisha Walker
Banner Created by: Krystal Wings
May 18, 2011: The opening of the Sean Elijah Bell Community Center

Photo Credit: Kisha Walker

May 18, 2011: The opening of the Sean Elijah Bell Community Center

Photo Credit: Kisha Walker

May 18, 2011: The opening of the Sean Elijah Bell Community Center

Photo Credit: Valerie Bell
Sean in the outfield on high school baseball team

Photo Credit: Valerie Bell
"Many Faces"

Photo Credit: Valerie Bell
The Bell family at Valerie's 50th birthday party, the
last family get-together before Sean's death

Chapter Eight

Thank You

In Faith and Thanksgiving

Giving thanks to our Lord and Savior Jesus Christ, only through Him am I able to endure this trial and tribulation, leaning my entire being on Him, beholding my salvation of rest. He lightens the burdens of my sorrow. I'm humbly thankful for the unshakable foundation of family support that surrounds me, a foundation of love that has fixed itself under my feet, holding me up and continuing with me in every step that I take. I love you all. My husband, who completes me and who has completed my circle of love and strength, thank you. Thank you for going before me yet not going over me in times of public appearances, and the many other new responsibilities that have entered our lives. I love you, Bud.

William Jr. and Delores, you are the only two children I have left. Thank you for wiping my tears. I value you both beyond emotions. My friends, I can't begin to thank you enough for your sacrifice of time and the support you've given to the family. This is truly one of the most devastating and challenging times in our lives. Having you all here portrays a magnitude of love to us. Thank you all.

Having faith as small as a mustard seed, I believe justice will prevail. Our son, our beautiful son Sean, the one the world has come to know as Sean Bell, will always be Sean to me. I miss him desperately. Countless times I've tried to bring forth my own understanding only to be humbled by the weight of my own thoughts. In silent love I wait for the day, and I continue to have faith that

**God will always get the glory
while Sean Elijah Bell gets his rightful story**

In enduring love,
Valerie M. Bell

A Special Thank You from the Bell Family

On behalf of the Bell family, we would like to express our heartfelt thanks and sincere gratitude to so many of you who have expressed your kindness and love in the home-going of our son, Sean Elijah Bell.

We are able unable to express or articulate the pain and agony that we feel as we grieve the loss of our son. As a mother, I will never again hold my son. Sean and his father will never have another father-son conversation. It is by the grace of God, who is the pillar of strength, that we have gotten through this.

Although our son will be gravely missed, his life and legacy will live on through his family. Sean was a wonderful and loving son, and every day we thank God for blessing us with him. We ask that you continue to pray for our strength in the Lord as we fight for justice and peace. When he was with us, our son never said good-bye. He always said, "See you later." We know we have this assurance that we will see our son later.

"I am the resurrection of life. He who believes in Me, though he may die, he shall live. And whoever lives and believes in Me shall never die." John 11:25

Sincerely,
The Bell Family
William, Valerie, William Jr., Delores,
Jada, and Jordyn

Acknowledgments

This *poetic memoir* would not have been possible without my team and the support from the relationships forged within the seven-year process of the creation of this book. My expression of gratitude is not without sincerity to those who read the manuscript and gave constructive feedback. I am fortunate to have received the favor of those who contributed to the book with written thoughts and/or photos.

Lastly, I would like to acknowledge Mr. George Taggert. Every morning during our fifty-day vigil George drove me to the vigil site, making sure I arrived exactly at 4:56 am, which was the exact time of Sean's death. Shortly after, George passed away. Our hearts were saddened yet thankful for having met such a giving and brave soul, an angel in the midst of our pain.

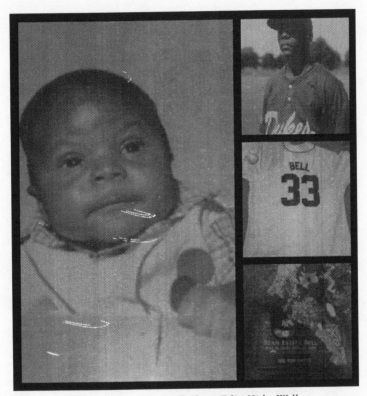

Photo Credit: Valerie Bell **Photo Edit**: Kisha Walker

"See You Later"

About the Author

Photo Credit: Kisha Walker

In the early morning hours of November 25, 2006, a mother was jolted out of her sleep by a phone call bearing the news that her son was in the hospital. Hours later, she would be forced to embrace the cruel reality of the circumstances surrounding his untimely death. Her son, Sean Bell, was killed in a hail of fifty shots fired by New York City police officers on his wedding day. He was just twenty-three. The sudden transition from the private life of motherhood to the very public position of being the mother of the late Sean Bell was intimidating to say the least, yet Valerie Bell emerged with a distinguished poise of grace, a disposition she credits to her faith in the Lord Jesus Christ.

Regarded as the "Ambassador for Justice" by her husband, William Bell Sr., Valerie Bell immersed herself as a committed contender in the fight against police brutality. The summer of 2014 highlighted the crimson stain of America's refusal to respond to the outcries of grieving mothers who were left desolate from the vehement effects of police brutality. Ferguson, Missouri's, impassioned lamentation over the killing of an unarmed eighteen-year-old male, Michael Brown, elevated to the height of the world stage, became the focal point of the movement against the long-existing racial divide in America. In the midst of it all, another mother was left to grieve.

Valerie Bell and Sabrina Fulton (the mother of Trayvon Martin) comforted Lesley McSpadden (the mother of Michael Brown) in the fragile days before her son was to be laid to rest. The trio of mothers, meeting for the first time in an exclusive interview with CNN, was affectionately nicknamed "The Sisterhood" by CNN anchor Don Lemon. In the interview, Valerie shared with Lesley McSpadden the key points of strength that have helped her move forward in her healing process. "You have to keep your head up, no matter what is done. Keep your head up."

As the climate of America continued to hover at its boiling point, Valerie Bell, along with nine other mothers who lost their sons to police brutality, traveled to Washington DC to take part in a Mothers' delegation (hosted by

Mothers Against Police Brutality, CODE PINK, National Congress of Black Women, and Hands Up DC Coalition). In the Congressional briefing on Capital Hill, Valerie Bell addressed the issue of the lack of police accountability.

In the days to follow, Valerie Bell took part in the "Millions March NYC" on December 13, 2014. Alongside other families who were victims of police brutality, Valerie Bell, holding onto the "Black Lives Matter" banner at the head of the march that numbered over 25,000 strong, marched as the voice of her son Sean Bell. In a written statement, Valerie Bell expressed the passion behind her participation in the march: "I march in solidarity at the 'Millions March NYC' protest in resistance to the genocidal mentality of police officers towards the people of our country. Lifting my voice with the protesters here today was extremely important."

Valerie Bell is no stranger to the opposition of injustice. Within the last eight years she has been embattled with challenges from adversarial agendas. The outcome of her efforts have been encrusted into the legendary history of New York City. In 2010, the New York City Council voted to designate Liverpool Street from 94th Avenue to 101st Avenue in Queens, the street where New York City police officers took Sean's life, as Sean Bell Way. It was a bittersweet victory for the Bell family.

A year later, on May 18, 2011, the Sean Elijah Bell Community Center opened its doors to the community, providing a safe haven for cultural and educational programs. The center provided service for more than 150 children and adults during its operation. After two years of serving the community, the Sean Elijah Bell Community Center closed its doors on November 22, 2013. In a statement referring to the center's closure, Valerie Bell encourages the community, "Above our hope is the Lord's will. Where He leads we will continue to follow. Our hearts are steadfast towards the advancement and well being of our community. We will be present and continue to help in anyway we can."

Valerie has worked with the Justice Committee and alongside other mothers who are fighting for justice against police brutality, with the agenda of securing an executive order signed by the governor establishing a special prosecutor for all cases of police killings within the Attorney General's Office. The position of the special prosecutor will eliminate the systemic issue of biased interest due to their close working relation with the Police Department; when district attorneys prosecute these cases. On March 11, 2015, Valerie Bell gave an emotional testimony before the New York State Assembly Standing Committees on Codes and Judiciary and the Black, Hispanic, Puerto Rican, and Asian Legislative Caucus, in a Hearing on Criminal Justice. On July 8, 2015, Governor Andrew Cuomo signed Executive Order No. 147, appointing the New York State Attorney General as a special prosecutor in matters relating to the deaths of unarmed civilians caused by on-duty law enforcement officers.

As a caterpillar knows the time to prepare for its metamorphosis, Valerie Bell also knew it was time for her to heal. Beginning her process towards healing and soul peace, Valerie has chosen to write the echoing of her heart in her first book, titled, SEAN BELL: Just 23. In her poetic memoir, Valerie gives a reflective account of the final days of her son Sean Bell and the subsequent agony of a mother's grieving heart.

This is a new beginning for Valerie Bell. The Lord has elucidated His purpose for her, and His calling has been made sure. Police brutality will one day be annihilated; until then, Valerie Bell will continue to be the "Voice for Sean."

Valerie Bell has been married for thirty-seven years to her teenage sweetheart, William G. Bell Sr. Their union brought forth three children: William G. Bell Jr., the late Sean E. Bell, and Delores J. Bell. She has three grandchildren, Jada and Jordyn Bell and Jalia Bell.

Author contact information: VBelljust23@gmail.com

About the Co-Author

Kisha Walker
Kisha Walker currently resides in New York.
The mother of two credits her gift to the Almighty God.
Co-Author contact information: KWalkerPublishing@gmail.com

Printed in the United States
By Bookmasters